Grandmothe

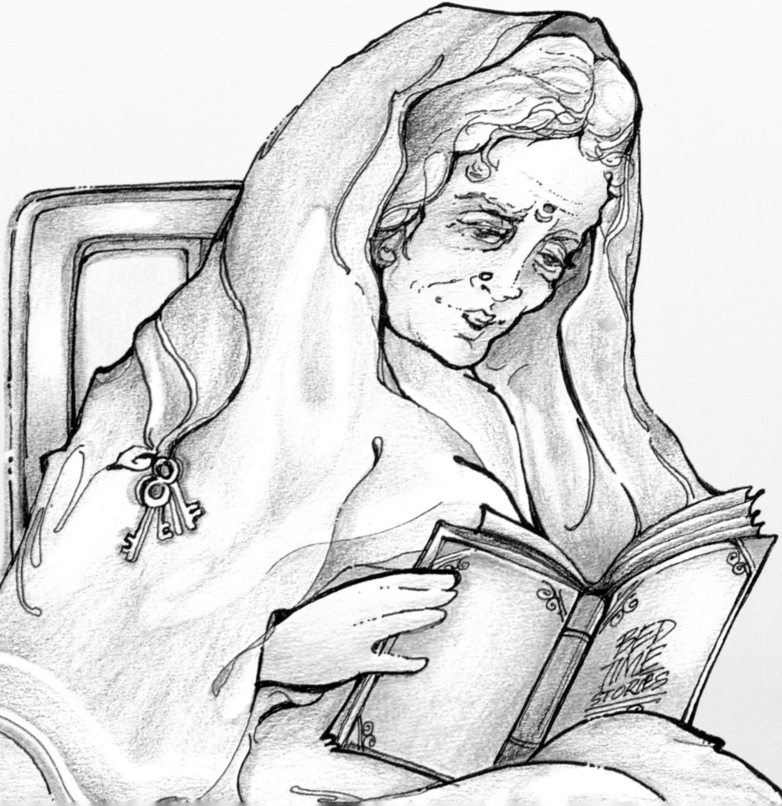

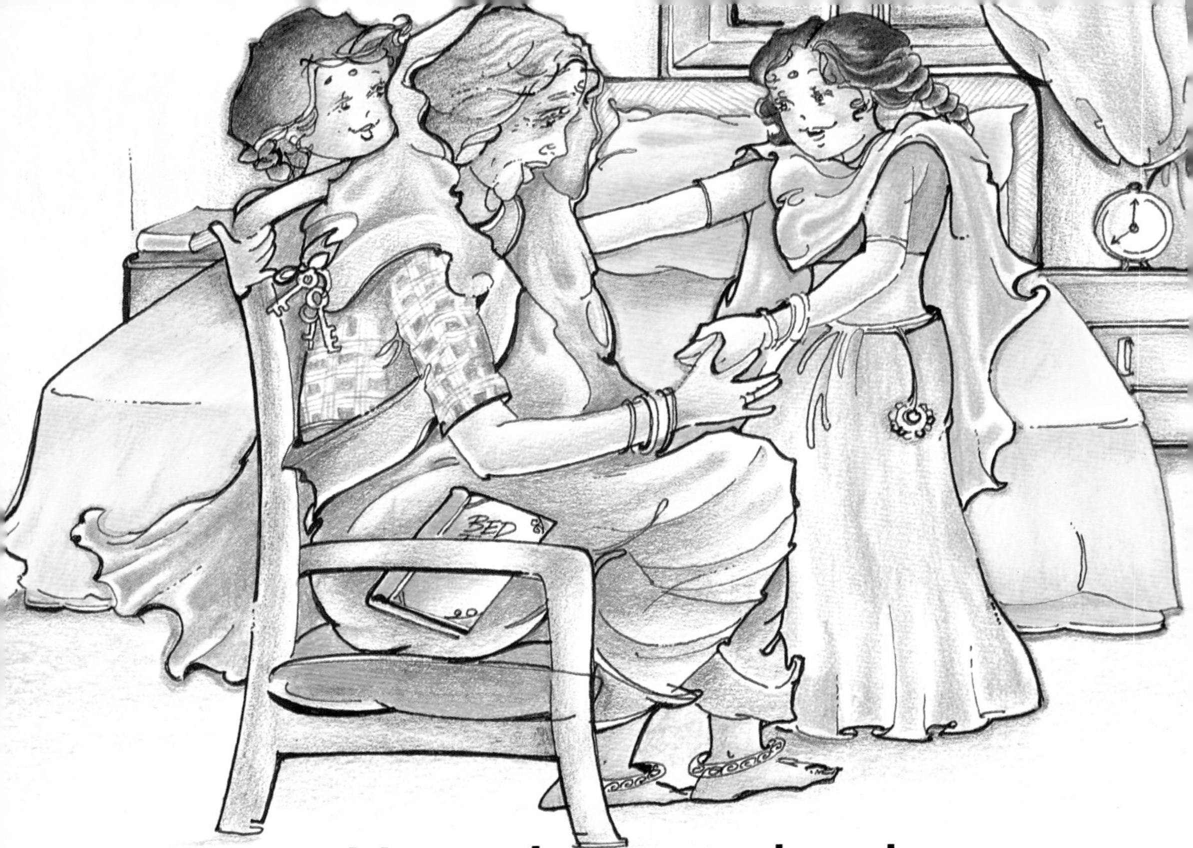

Here is your bed,
grandmother.

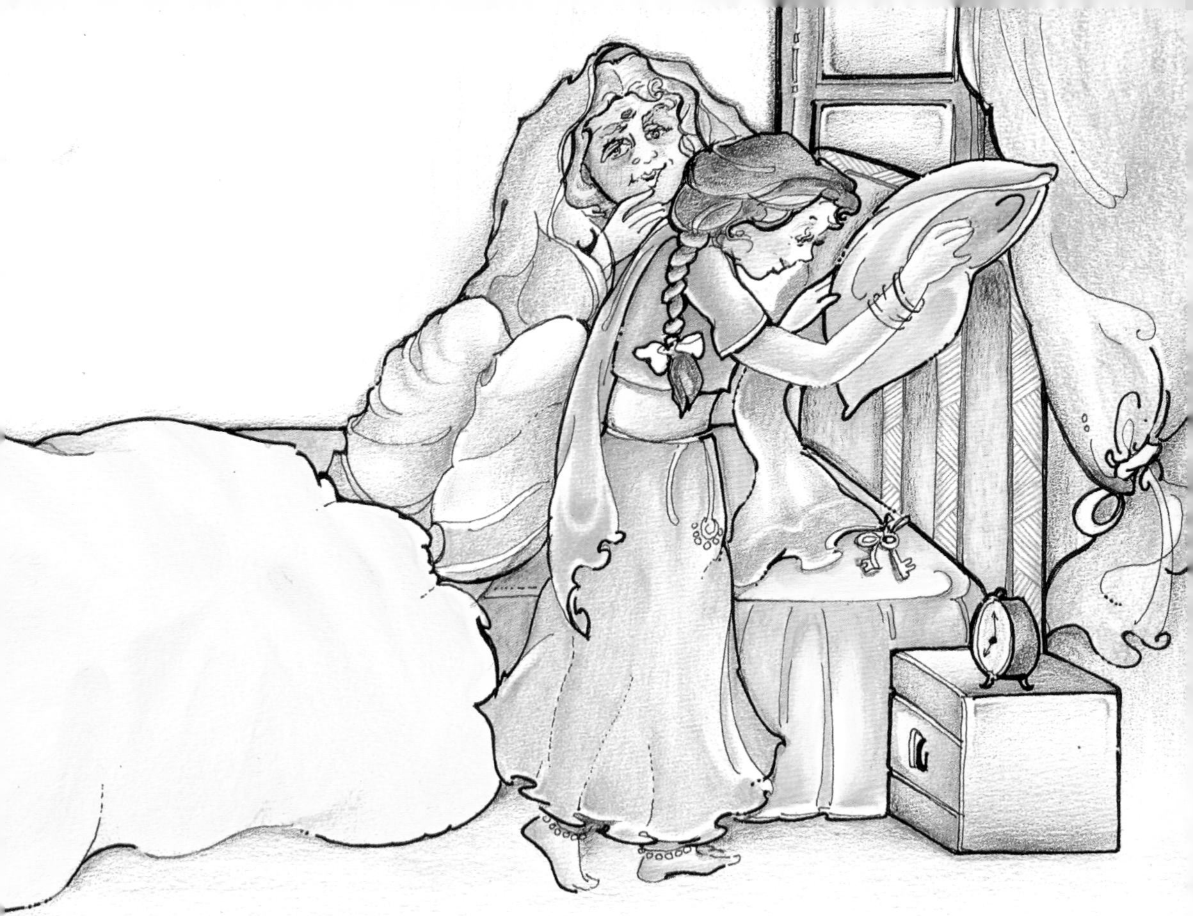

Here is your pillow.

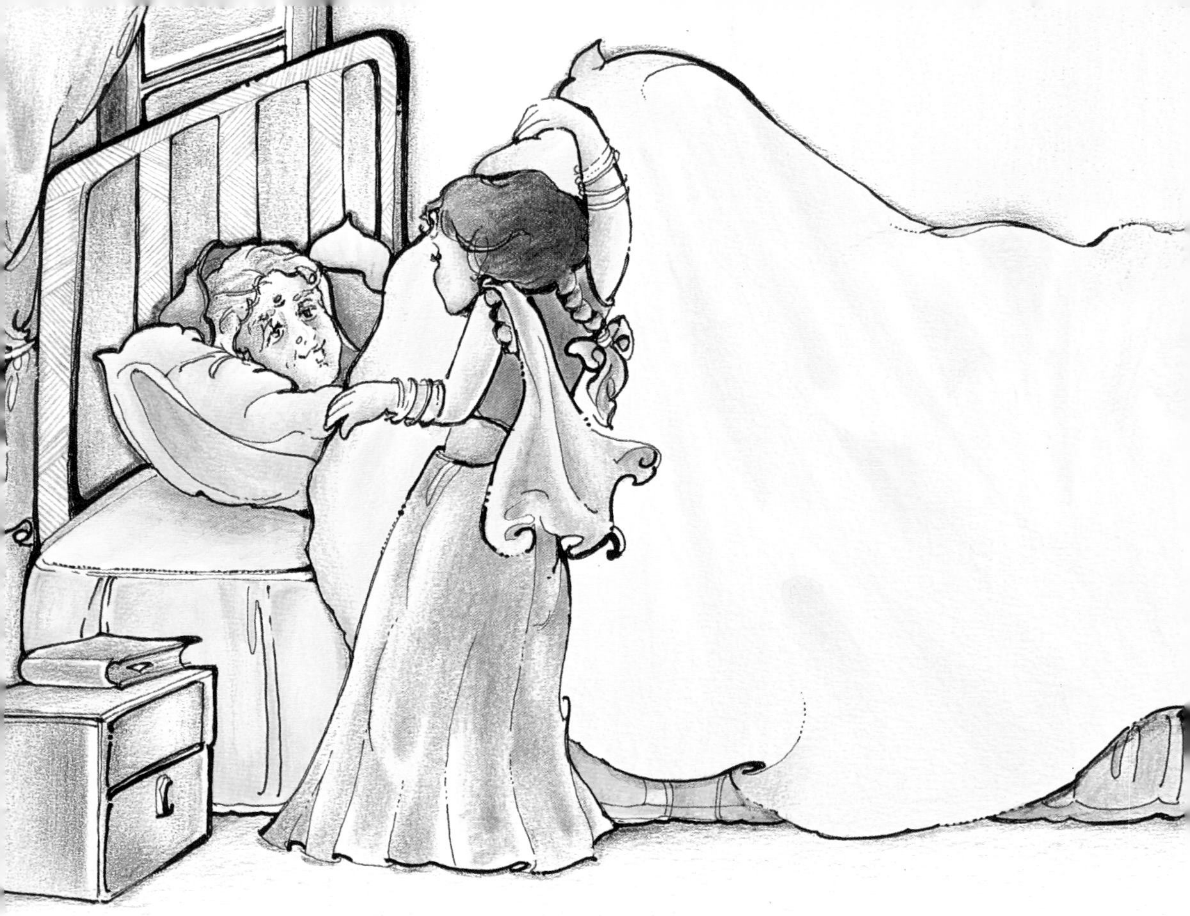

Here is your blanket.

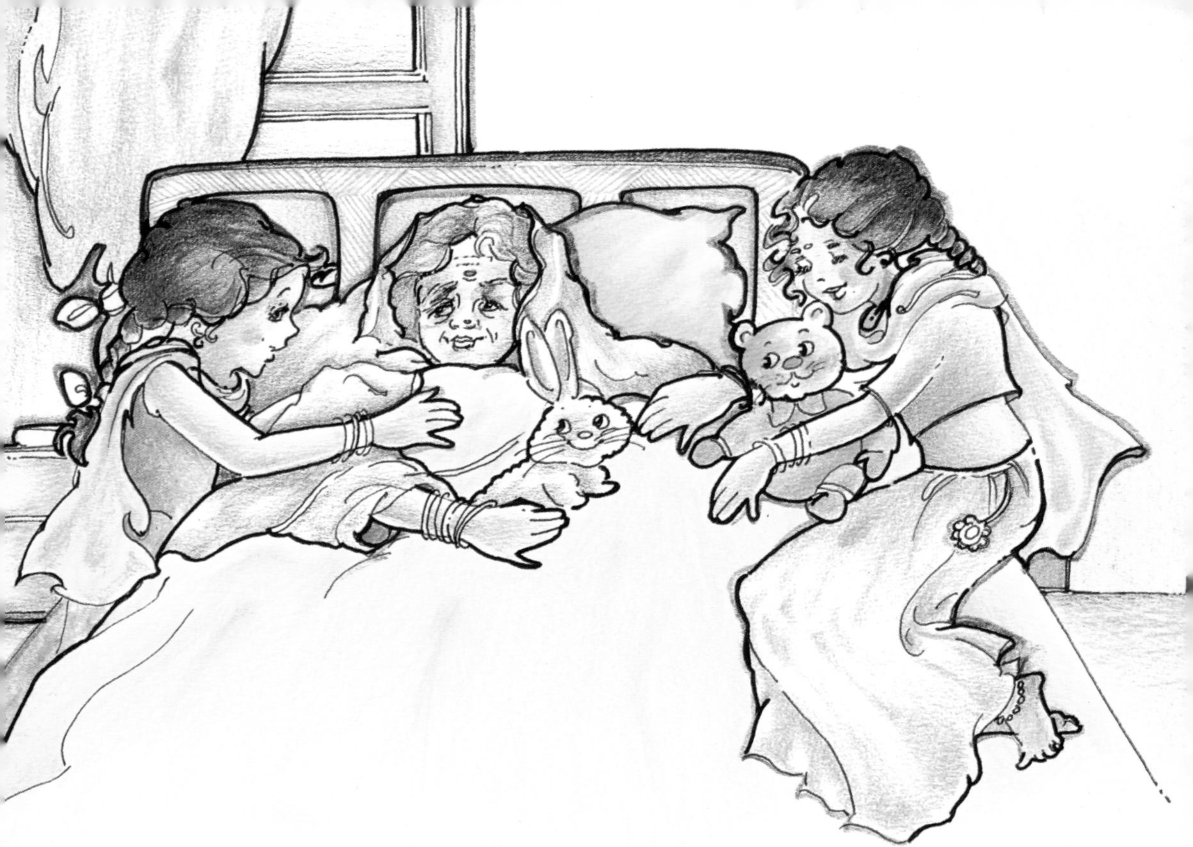

Here is a rabbit and a bear.

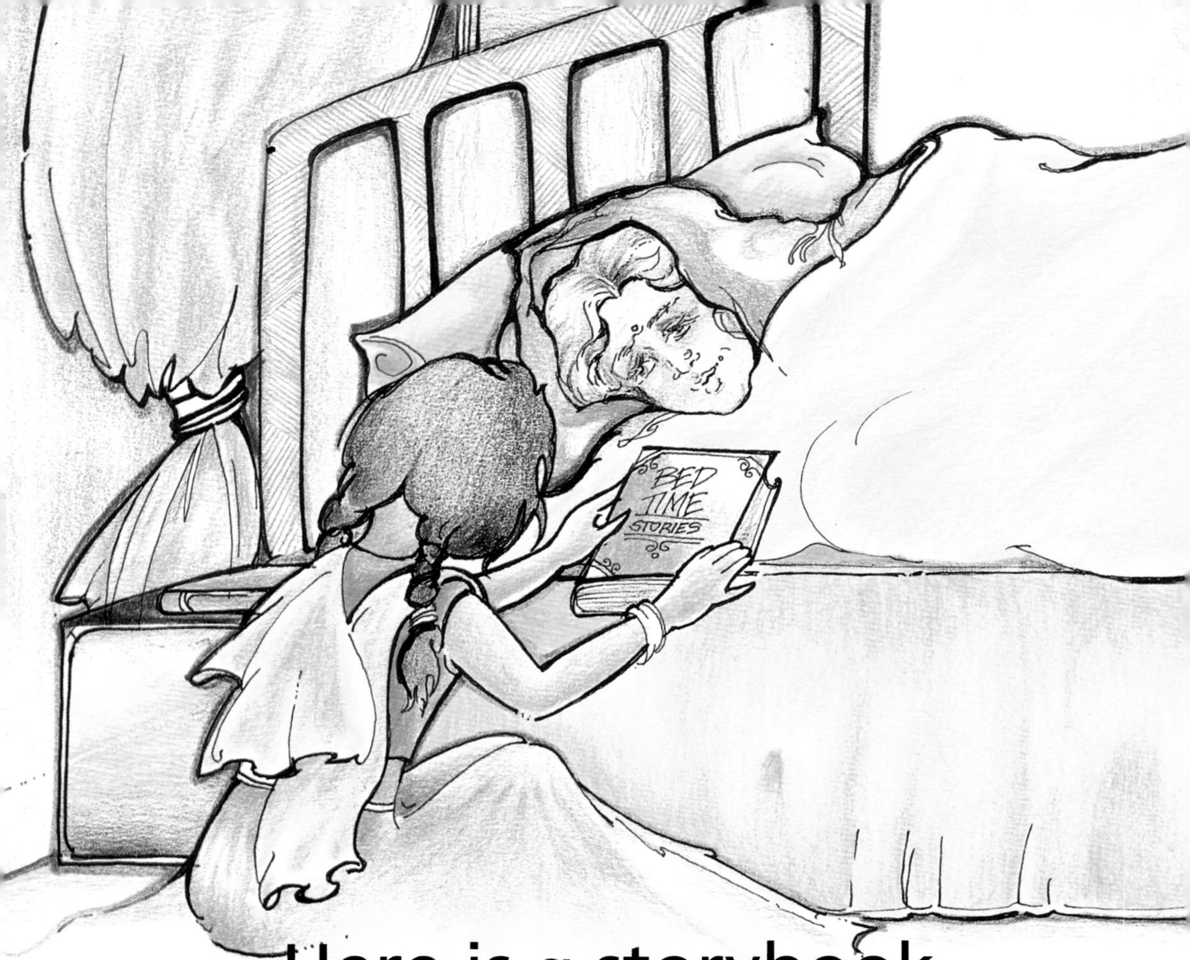

Here is a storybook.

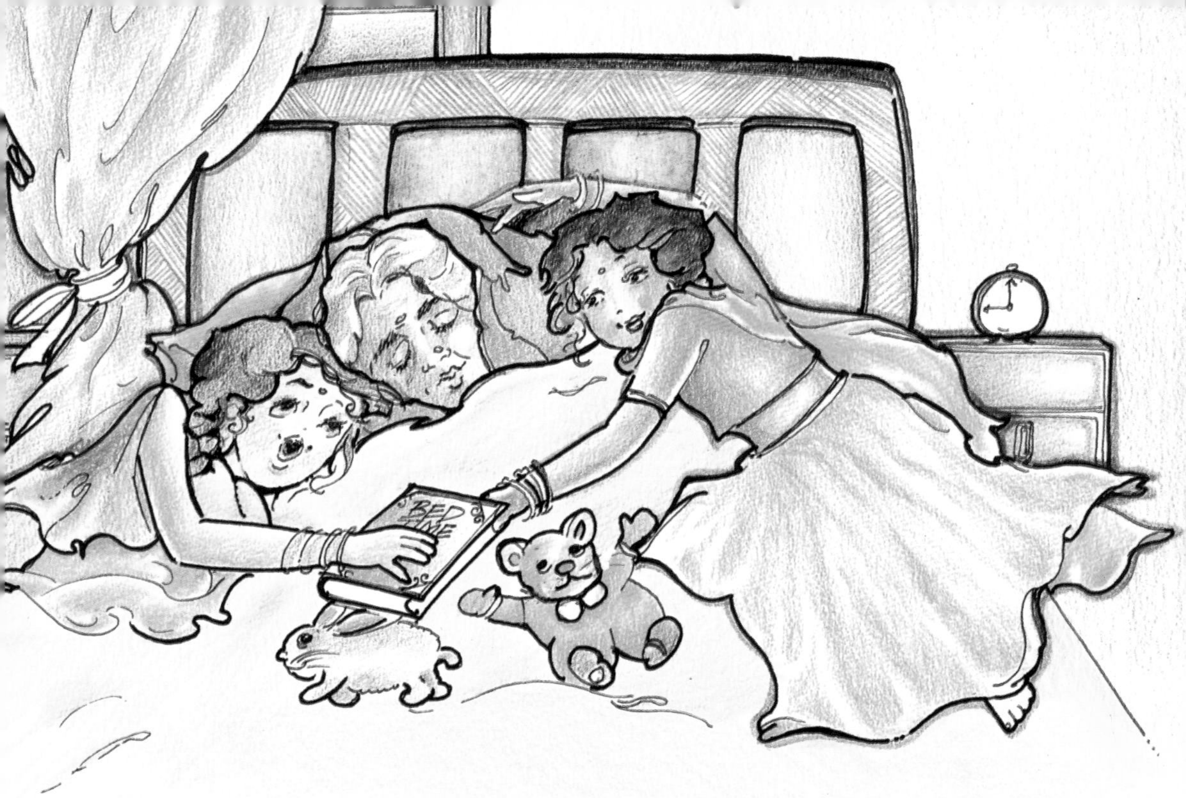

We are tired, too.

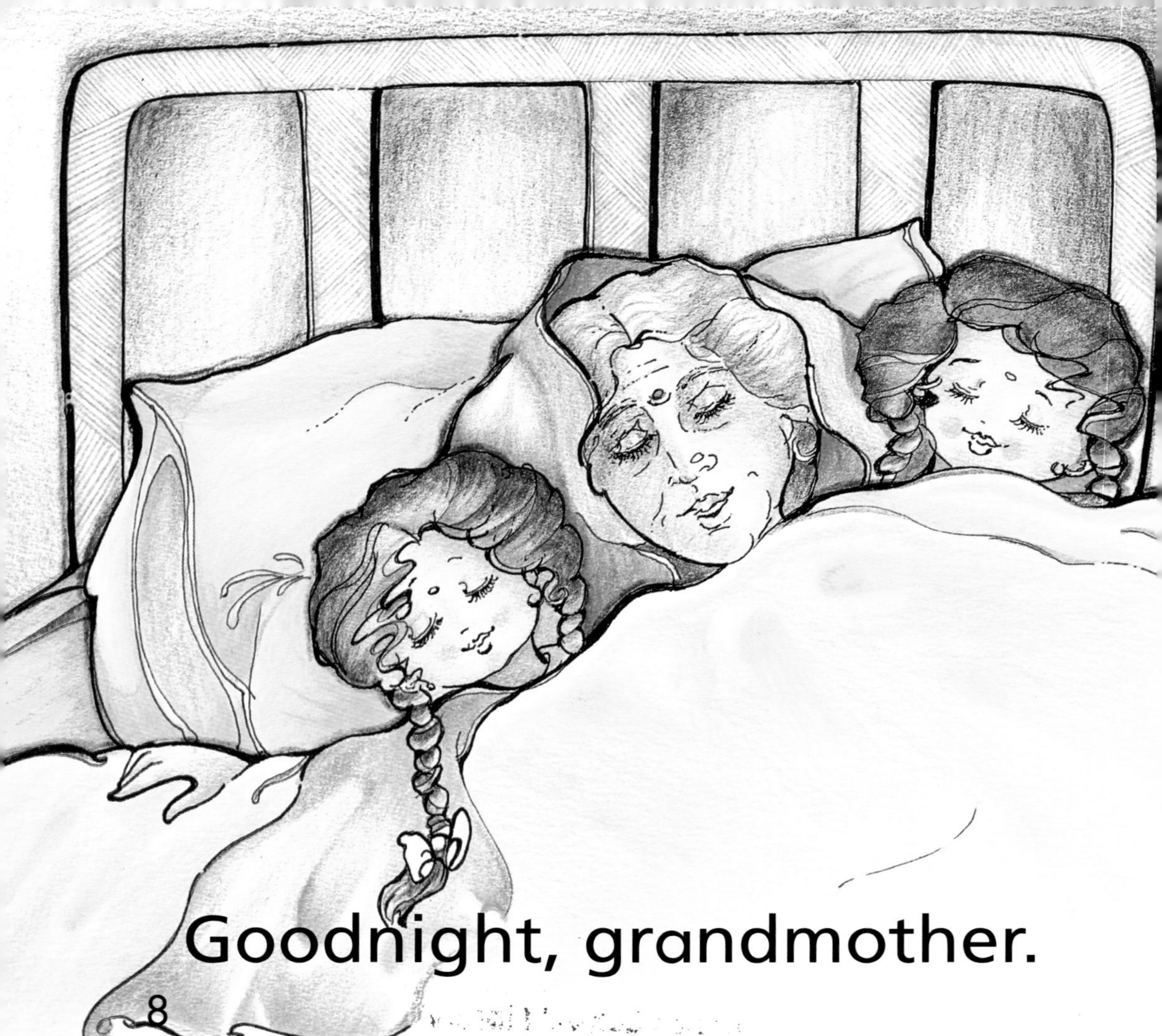

Goodnight, grandmother.